SKEWED VIEWS

THE DITZY CARTOONS OF
Roy Schlemme

ISBN: 0-7596-9336-6

Library of Congress Number: 2002090238

This book is printed on acid free paper.

Printed in the United States of America
Bloomington, IN

1st Books - rev. 5/29/02

"Laugh if you will,
but firm young thoraxes still excite me."

And hopefully, there'll be plenty to excite and delight you in
this hilariously twisted view of a world gone buggy. A great escape,
"Skewed Views" will take you to such fun places you'll wish
the tour would never end. It begins with a meander through Droll, Witty
and Urbane. From there you'll wend your way through Farcical, Jocular,
Rascally and Playful (I'd add more adjectives, but my thesaurus broke.).
After finishing the Grand Tour, feel free to tell your friends
how much you enjoyed the trip.
Bon voyage.

—Roy Schlemme

"Here, Arlo. You'll feel better
once you've had a little grub."

"And remember, it's not for you to decide
what 'The Angel of Death' should look like."

"Your looping letterforms indicate an expansive
character. The strong cross-strokes show great tenacity,
and writing on my tablecloth rather than a piece of paper
tells me you're dumber than stone."

"It's been a long time out here for you, hasn't it, Fred?"

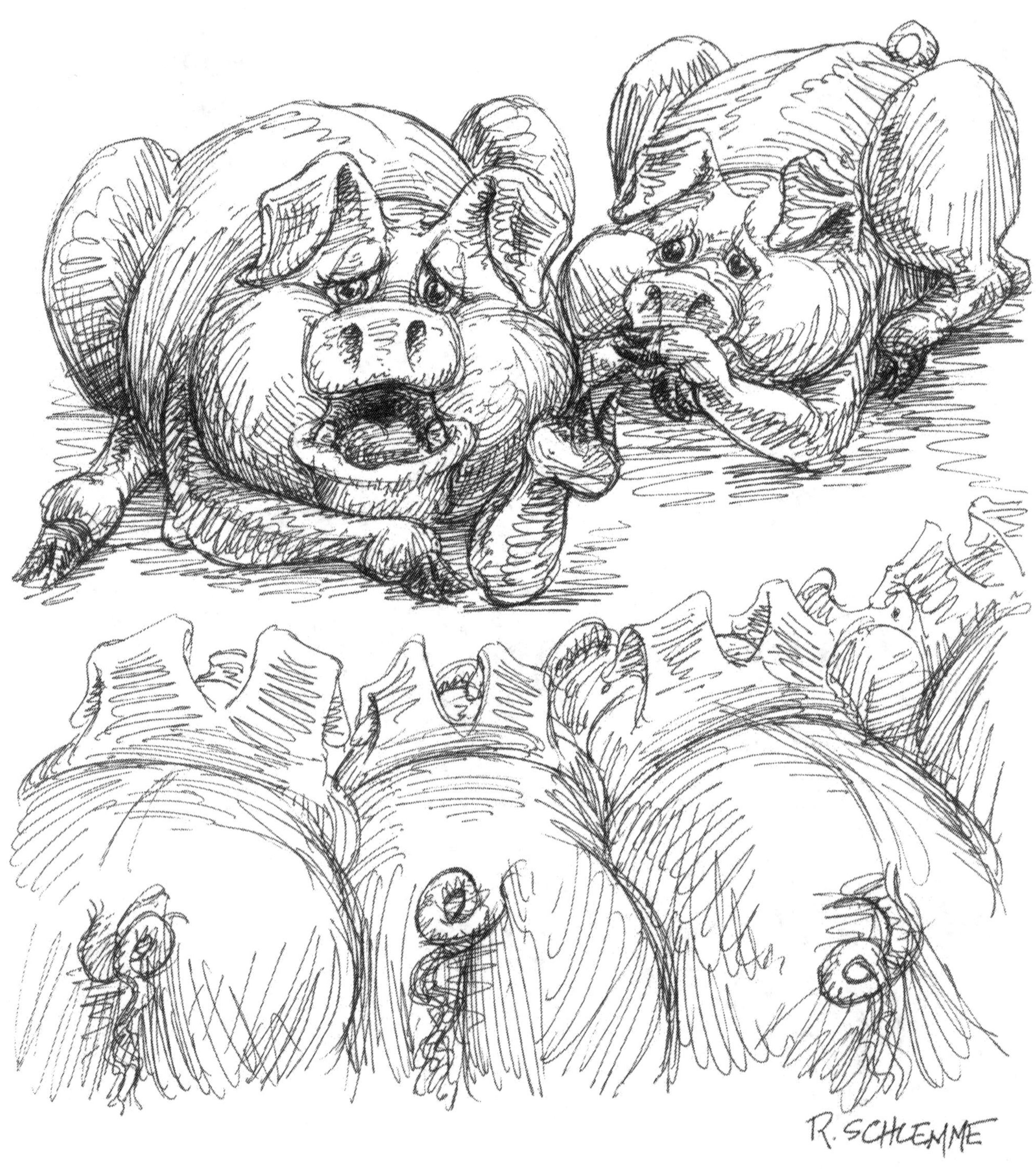

"She says we're all about to be butchered.
I think that's a load of baloney."

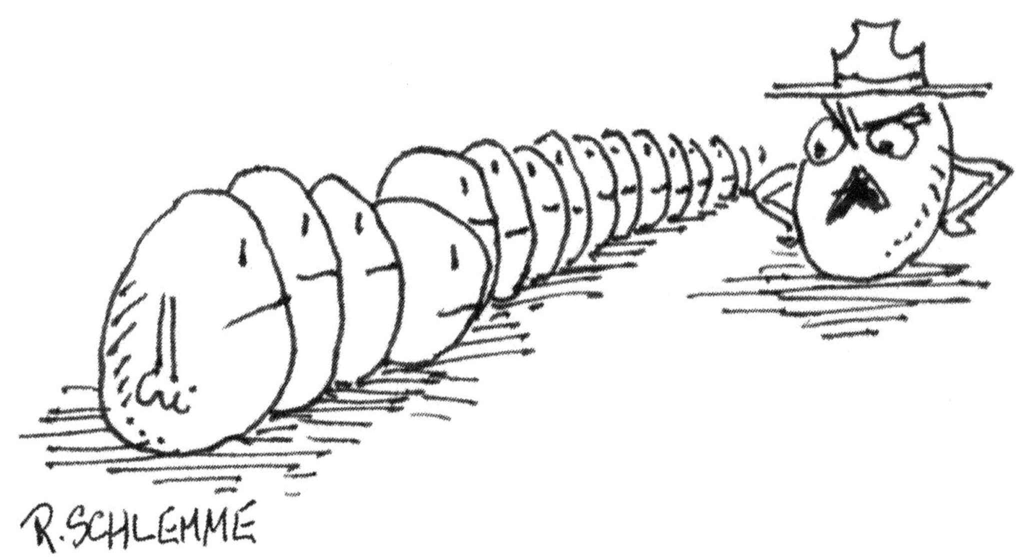

"Number 4, suck in that yolk!"

"O Great Spirit, give us a sign in this hour of decision.
How many roulette tables shall we install?"

"The translation reveals one of their more feisty pharaohs. It reads, 'Touch my tomb and your ass is grass!'."

"As for those not named 'Ratso',
go back to bed. Everything's under control."

PLEASE HELP!
TRYING TO MAKE IT ON MY OWN!
R. SCHLEMME

COCKTAIL WIENERS
R. SCHLEMME

Nutrition Facts
Serving size: .1 oz.
Calories: 0
% Daily Value
Total Fat 0g 0%
Saturated Fat 0g 0%
Sodium 0g 0%
Carbohydrates 0g 0%
Fiber 0g 0%
Sugars 0g 0%
Protein 0g 0%
No food value whatsoever.
R. SCHLEMME

WELCOME TO HELL!
R. SCHLEMME

William Penn and the Quackers

"Two things, Denise...Your blind date's here
and don't bother wearing heels."

"Not planning anything un-Tarzan-like are we?"

"Hi! We're all out of today's paper, but if you've got
about three minutes, I can do a quick recap."

Song of the Aussie Vikings

Returning from Little League, Bobby froze
at the front door. Something was in the house...
and it was waiting for him!

"Oh, they're fine.
The young prince is teaching
Esmarelda how to play poker."

"Take a bit off the sides, keep the top
fairly full and don't touch the braid."

"So he thinks he can still down jalapeños whole...
Gentlemen, start your engines!"

TREASURES
OF
LASCAUX

"Nobody is <u>that</u> perfect!"

"You'll notice how when the facets catch
light in just the right way, you can see
Dippy the Hippo saying, 'Hi!'."

"Following graduation, I worked a few years in the theater industry.
After that I spent some time with a flag company until
landing my current job at the sheriff's office."

"Hoppenfeld, the post office doesn't need cheap theatrics
to market its new commemoratives."

Wendell, conscientious and unsuspecting,
was about to run afoul of the old
'Tarantula on the Inspection Belt' gag.

Organized crime

"It's awfully hard to get ticked
at a beanballer who's that sensitive."

"I perceive a faint beam
of light...growing...growing..."

"Our problem is we look
too damn eater-friendly."

"Unfortunately, sir, 'Is it still raining outside?'
wanders from the general trend of questioning
we're trying to develop here."

R. SCHLEMME

"Just once, I'd like to feel there's someone
left in the world who can spell."

"As the old adage goes,
'Either you fly the cherub or the cherub flies you'."

SOCKET TO ME!
200W 80V
R. SCHLEMME
Current Lightweight Champ
EAT MY SLIME!
I ACCELERATE FOR FRENCH CHEFS.
GASTROPOD PRIDE ON THE MOVE!
R. SCHLEMME

Suddenly Billy Joe remembered Old Hank's warning,
'Don't wear squeaky boots if you're entered in
The Brahma Bull Tail Pull!'

"I see everybody's in this morning."

"Officer, don't you think a mother knows
if one of her children is missing?"

Vi was basically happy,
in spite of having married into a family with
the longest Polish surname in the world.

Before the first cow/chicken dictionary

MAD HORNETS
MARCHING
BAND
R. SCHLEMME

DR. MAIZE
EAR PROBLEMS
R. SCHLEMME

"Stop the ceremony! The groom is cracked!"

"Run, Ella Mae!
The aliens have landed!"

Mothers' Day portrait.

"I hate serving in a peacetime army!"

"Yes, it's your imagination.
They're both exactly the same size."

"Nope, family's been drinkin' this river water
for generations with nary a problem."

"I don't respond well to
deities with dirty fingernails!"

HIT THIS SIGN
AND WIN A FREE
ANGLO-SAXON
PRINCESS!
R. SCHLEMME

Unable to find the pocket calculator, Mindy once again
revealed her shortcomings in trajectory math to both
'Whammo the Great' and a sorely disappointed sellout crowd.

"I don't care what you remember.
Bitchiness was never one of *The Seven Deadly Sins*."

"Did you have to ask 'Which one is Zeppo?'?"

"I remember when things really used to hop around here."

"Rainbow! Rainbow!"

"Bear left, hairball, bear left!"

"Well, now...who'd like to start off and
talk a bit about their problems with sunlight?"

"What looks good for appeasing a wrathful God?"

"...and now she's taking off the black lace bra..."

"I fly into history."

"I think I've hit my tippy-tap limit."

"We're all the unopened junk mail that
you've ever thrown away, Mr. Davidson;
only this time around, you'll be dealing with us."

THIS MONTH'S
"FRIENDS OF
THE CARPET"
MEETING
TO BE HELD IN APT 8B'S
BLUE SHAG WEAVE!
BRING THE LITTLE ONES!
ALL THE VIRGIN WOOL
YOU CAN EAT!
R. SCHLEMME

"Now go out there and make
a great fool of yourself."

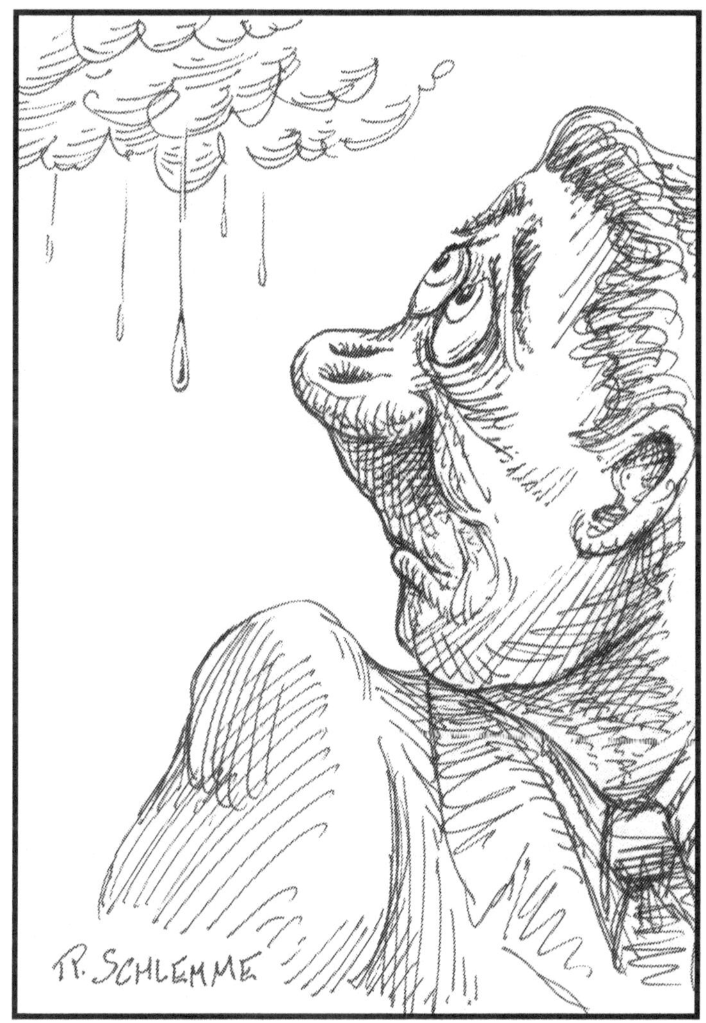

Looking up, Quinby was
seized by his greatest fear—
it was beginning to rain.

How to prepare
Louis XVI Egg Salad:
<u>Step No. 1</u>

"It fell out of the sky one day
and somebody said, 'This must be a sign!'.
Then one thing just led to another."

"Ooooo!...and what's this cute little fork for?"

"Hey, if it wasn't for a few hypercritical fringe groups,
I'd be first in line to book a frozen cat juggler."

R. SCHLEMME

THE WORM FARM UPRISING
BOTH SIDES
TELL WARDEN, WE AIN'T GONNA EAT ANY MORE OF THIS GARBAGE.
IT'S GOTTEN TOTALLY OUT OF HAND. SEND IN THE ROBINS!!
R. SCHLEMME

"Look here, Watson. We simply follow this slime trail
and our giant snail, although a master of disguise, is cornered."

"Looks like their weapons technology goes
well beyond anything we've come up with."

"Fortunately, you no longer think you're a birdhouse.
However, I'd hesitate telling them until the nesting season's over."

"I still can't fathom why the pet store
was so reluctant to sell us that adorable kitty
just because it was a whiner."

"The noise is almost deafening,
especially around the holidays."

HONK IF YOU HATE MIGRATING!
R. SCHLEMME

BY READING THIS DISTRACTING BILLBOARD THERE'S A GOOD CHANCE YOU'LL MESS UP ON THE HIDDEN CURVE JUST AHEAD AND SKID INTO THE BUSIEST INTERSECTION WITHIN A THREE COUNTY RADIUS.
THIS MESSAGE IN THE PUBLIC INTEREST BROUGHT TO YOU BY
BERNIE'S AUTO TOW & REPAIR 367-1107
R. SCHLEMME

"Carol, when you've finished,
Mr. Kong is here for his pedicure."

Wild Elephant Survival Skills School

"That's very nice, Mr. Mumbly, but it's your walking we'd prefer to focus on."

The problem with centipedes as an audience
is that you can never really know
how many enjoyed the performance.

"C'mon, Jerry. Just let me call them for the right phrasing."

"So where is mama's birthday boy
hiding himself now?"

Politically-correct
SWAT team sharpshooter

"Happily Ms. Grackle, modern orthopedics
does have an answer for little bowed legs."

"Quick, check and see if the crew
is up for some squid tonight."

"I see Jellybelly finally got that liposuction!"

"O.K., now watch this one, 'Baste, Rex! Baste!'."

Sports equipment tomfoolery

"Can any of you fully appreciate the difficulty
in dealing with dense vegetation?"

People driven by the cats in their lives

"Don't jiggle your Jell-o at me, mister!"

"Normally, I'd roust him down from there,
but the townsfolk really seem to enjoy that
special sound of bone against bronze."

"Tell Big George to stop looking. I found 'em!"

"The boomers are coming! The boomers are coming!"

Revenge of the Cantata Flies

"There's one that looks like a
cumulonimbus with a little party hat."

"C'mon, Lloyd. Not everything's
a competitive challenge."

"I find your garish display sickening!"

PALACE
HORROR SHOW DOUBLE FEATURE
RAIN AND
THE SUN ALSO RISES
R. SCHLEMME

DIGNITY WITHOUT GOBBLING!
R. SCHLEMME

"Roll over, Rex, me lad...
or it'll be a taste of the cat for thee!"

"I see it as my first of many
grand architectural statements!"

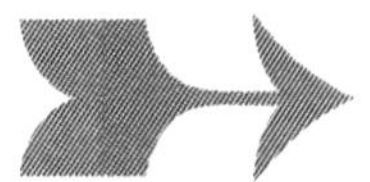

If Thomas Edison had not developed his language skills fully...

"Sorry to intrude, but we've been getting
a slight gas odor in 9-E."

"So, you call it bulletproof glass, eh, da Vinci?
And what exactly is a bullet?"

to the Falls

STAY ON PATH.
WINKELMAN'S FALLS 1.8 M (3K)

CANOES + HIKING GEAR FOR HIRE
SEE SAM AT CREEKSIDE
WINKELMAN'S FALLS
THE STORY OF NATURE'S UNBRIDLED BEAUTY
STATE FORESTRY SVC.

NOW OPEN
CABINS AVAILABLE!
DAILY OR WEEKLY RATES
WINKELMAN'S IN-THE-WOODS
TAKE THE PLUNGE !!!
HOURLY TOURS OF OUR ROARING FALLS!
SNACKS & SOUVENIRS AT THE HISTORIC BOATHOUSE

WINK'S LODGE
CHEZ JERKY (WILDERNESS CUISINE)
GREAT VIEW THE FALLS
DAY KAMP FOR KIDS
POLO FIELD
HANG GLIDING
TENNIS COURTS
GOLF COURSE
ROLLER COASTER
SAUNA

THE GRAND "W"
HOTEL & CASINO
OPEN 24 HRS. A DAY
FLOOR SHOWS NIGHTLY IN OUR FABULOUS NATTY BUMPO ROOM
THIS WEEK: "MAIDENS ALONG THE MOHAWK!"
THE GRAND "W" 3-D THEATER
NOW PLAYING
OUR WILD LAND
SEE A MILLION YEARS OF NATURAL EVOLUTION IN OUR 30-MINUTE VIRTUAL REALITY SWOOP-O-SCOPE PRESENTATION
THE OLD FALLS

R. SCHLEMME

"No problem, ma'am. It's only one of
those little Peruvian folk groups that seems
to pop up in the most unexpected places."

"All I recall from the interview was
him saying, 'I want you on my team.'."

"Too much lemon extract?"

"And finally, just before shooting,
remove the safety."

Marie Antoinette has some
functional remodeling done at Versailles.

"That piece would've sounded even better if we didn't stash our nuts in here, too."

"Big Bill, our research analyst, just came up with a couple of very interesting investment picks."

"Next New Year's Eve, I'll do the guest list."

"You find me greatly disadvantaged, Gaston."

"How's the bite down now?"

OH, GOD...NOW HE KNOWS
I EAT VICHYSSOISE
WITH MY HANDS!
R. SCHLEMME

TATTOOS FOR YOUSE
BOAS RULE
R. SCHLEMME

HOW THE WEST WAS WON.

1.

2.

3.
R. SCHLEMME

"Then there are some with a special talent
for making bad things worse."

"The organization frowns upon those members
who choose to forsake trumpeting."

"Hey, everybody, *Meals on Wheels* is here!"

"Pothole repair, please!"

"I definately sense a seller's market today!"

"Eeeeeeeeeeek!!!"

"Hey...hey! You guys forgot this thing again!"

"C'mon, Luke. It's never too late
to discover the leafy goodness of kale."

"And most special thanks for the return of Brother Claude
after his recent close call in the Brazilian jungles."

"Alright, you win!
Order the new diagnostic equipment!"

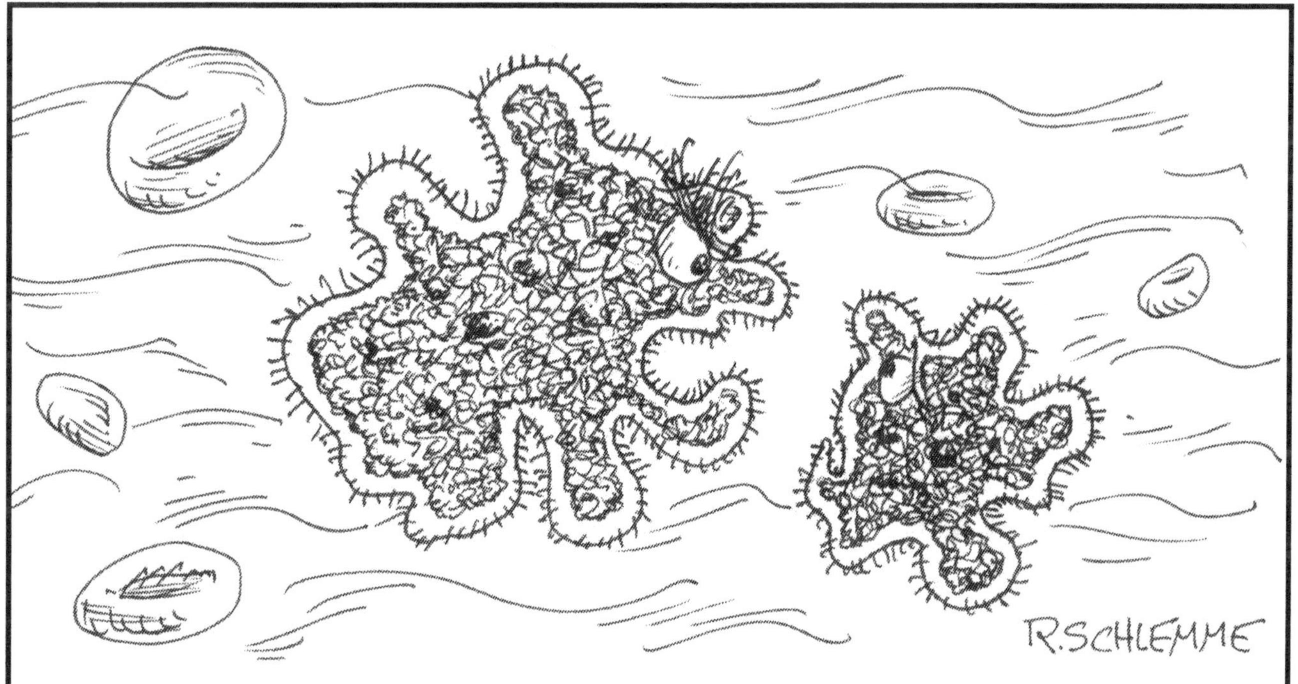

"Eat your platelets first,
or <u>no</u> <u>infection</u>!"

"Tiffany, we think you're old enough to be told!
You're adopted!"

"Oh, you choose! Something nice and romantic!"

"That's not a new extension on
the interstate, yew fool! It's a varicose vein!"

"Beard wedge, please."

JUSTICE TRIUMPHS!
R. SCHLEMME

The Lost Prediction of Nostradamus

"Your alpha male stare might
sell better from a vertical position."

"I can't examine if you don't peel."

Li'l Buckaroo Croquet

" Last one down turns off the tree."

Li'l Buckaroo Croquet injury time-out

The Art Critics

www.ingramcontent.com/pod-product-compliance
Lightning Source LLC
Chambersburg PA
CBHW080451030726
47592CB00011B/3072